TO MY LOVE

T0359733

TO MY LOVE

A LOVE LETTER TO PARENTHOOD

Jessica Urlichs and Sarah Reinhardt

I REMEMBER US, MY LOVE
WITH PLANS SO YOUNG AND FREE
OUR FACES FLUSH LIKE SPRINGTIME
WHEN IT WAS JUST YOU AND ME.

TIME SHINING LIKE DIAMONDS
BEFORE TURNING TO SAND.
HOLDING ON SO TIGHTLY
AS IT SLIPS RIGHT THROUGH OUR HANDS.

AND THROUGH THIS BEAUTIFUL BLUR
WE'LL WATCH OUR DREAMS COME TRUE.
AS BUSY AS OUR DAYS WILL BE,
OUR WORLD WILL STAND STILL TOO.

THE WOBBLY STEPS ARE OURS AT FIRST
WE STUMBLE AND WE FALL
AND AS THEIR WORLD GETS BIGGER
OURS IS SUDDENLY QUITE SMALL.

WE'RE IN A STORM AT SEA
TWO TIRED SHIPS AT NIGHT.
MUCH SMALLER THAN THE WAVES,
DRIFTING TOWARDS SUNLIGHT.

THROUGH THE FOG, THERE IS A GLOW,
A PERFECT LITTLE FACE.
SPRINKLING LIFE WITH MESS AND LOVE,
OUR STAR IN OUTER SPACE.

KICKING FEET AND SPONGY HANDS
DISTRACT FROM YOU AND I.
BUT THESE PRECIOUS DAYS ARE SHORT
AND THEY WILL QUICKLY PASS US BY.

AND THOUGH WE ARE STILL YOU AND I
THE WAY WE LOVE HAS CHANGED.
NOW OUR PUZZLE PIECES
ARE PERFECTLY ARRANGED.

SOME DAYS WE FEEL WILTED,
BUT WE'RE STEADY AND STRONG TOGETHER.
ALWAYS NURTURING OUR LOVE
AND FLOURISHING MORE THAN EVER.

POCKETS OF TIME OPEN UP,
WE SEE EACH OTHER MORE.
KISSES RUSHED, AND SOMETIMES MISSED,
AS WE HURRY OUT THE DOOR.

FLEETING MOMENTS IN THE EVENINGS,
ACROSS THE KITCHEN SINK,
LOTS TO SAY, YET NOTHING AT ALL,
TOO TIRED TO EVEN THINK.

THE COLOUR RETURNS TO OUR FACES,
THOUGH IT FADES FROM THE LIVING ROOM.
THEY ARE MY HOME, AND SO ARE YOU,
TOGETHER WE ALWAYS BLOOM.

THERE ARE NIGHTS WE STAY UP LATE,
FILLED WITH WORRY AND DOUBT.
THERE ARE DAYS WE DISAGREE,
AND WE'RE TWISTED INSIDE OUT.

THERE'S STILL SO MUCH TO JUGGLE,
SOMETIMES WE DROP THE BALL
THINGS MISSED AND THINGS FORGOTTEN,
BUT UNITED THROUGH IT ALL.

WE ARGUE AND WE BICKER,
BUT WE ALWAYS PUT THEM FIRST.
THEN, AT NIGHT, WE COUNT THE WAYS
THEY MAKE OUR HEARTS JUST BURST.

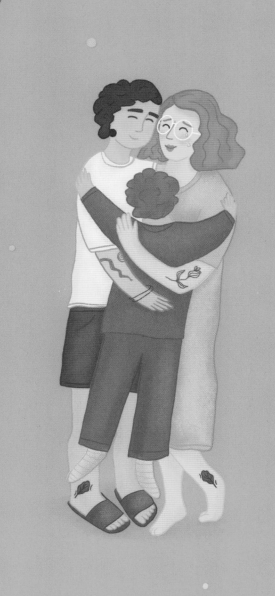

THE SACRIFICES THAT WE MAKE
AND THE THINGS WE PUT ASIDE,
ARE WORTH THE JOURNEY THAT WE'RE ON,
THIS BEAUTIFUL, BUMPY RIDE.

MAYBE IT'S ALL AS WE PLANNED,
OR MAYBE WE'VE LET GO
OF EVERYTHING WE THOUGHT WE KNEW
TO LOVE THIS LIFE WE KNOW.

I KNOW SOME DAYS YOU WONDER,
BECAUSE I FORGET TO SAY,
JUST HOW MUCH I SEE YOU,
AND LOVE YOU MORE EACH DAY.

SOMETIMES WE FEEL FAR APART,
AN OCEAN IN BETWEEN.
FIXING DOESN'T MEND A HEART
AS MUCH AS FEELING SEEN.

IN BETWEEN OUR LOVE FOR THEM,
WE SEE EACH OTHER TOO.
OUR LOVE IT SHOWS, EVERYDAY,
IN THE WONDERFUL THINGS THEY DO.

THEY TEACH US MORE ABOUT OURSELVES
AND OF COURSE, WE MAKE MISTAKES.
WE BUILD EACH OTHER UP
THROUGH ALL THE LESSONS AND THE BREAKS.

WE BORROW OUR SWEET BABIES
AND DAILY WATCH THEM GROW.
WE HOLD THEIR HANDS SO TIGHTLY,
SO ONE DAY THEY'LL LET GO.

AND AS THE YEARS CONTINUE,
EACH ENDING HAS A START.
WE SHINE WITH THEM, A FAMILY,
AND WE HAND THE WORLD OUR HEART.

THE EMPTY ROOMS, THE BUSY WALLS
OF FACES YOUNG AND OLD.
ON THE SOFA, YOUR HAND IN MINE,
A LOVE STORY STILL BEING TOLD.

BUT WE AREN'T THERE, MY LOVE, NOT YET.
WE HAVE CHAPTERS STILL TO WRITE.
WITH TEARS, LAUGHTER, LOVE AND STRENGTH
FOR AS LONG AS THE MOON SHINES BRIGHT.

BECAUSE ONE DAY WE'LL LOOK BACK
AT THIS BEAUTIFUL LIFE WE GREW,
SO LET'S REMEMBER YOU AND I.

TO MY LOVE,
MY ALWAYS,
TO YOU.

Jessica Urlichs

To my love, I'd live this life one
thousand times with you.

Jessica is a New Zealand poet
who has three children and
loves writing about the
ordinary being extraordinary.

Sarah Reinhardt

To all the ups and downs that
make us who we are; to my love.

Sarah is an illustrator who lives
full-time on the road with her
partner. Telling stories with her
illustrations is a dream come true.

Published in New Zealand in 2024 by Moa Press
(an imprint of Hachette New Zealand Limited)
Level 2, 23 O'Connell Street, Auckland, New Zealand
www.moapress.co.nz
www.hachette.co.nz

Text copyright © Jessica Urlichs 2024
Illustrations copyright © Sarah Reinhardt 2024

The rights of Jessica Urlichs and Sarah Reinhardt to be identified
as author and illustrator of this work have been asserted.
All rights reserved. No part of this publication may be
reproduced or transmitted in any form or by any means,
electronic or mechanical, including photocopying,
recording, or any information storage and retrieval system,
without the permission in writing from the publisher.

A catalogue record for this book is available
from the National Library of New Zealand.

978-1-86971-548-9 (hardback)

Cover and internal design by Sarah Reinhardt
Printed in China by Toppan Leefung Printing Ltd